A QUILTER'S GARDEN

A QUILTER'S GARDEN

—From Plants of the Holy Land—

HELEN SQUIRE

Fleming H. Revell Company
Old Tappan, New Jersey

Photo Credits

All photography by Myron Miller.

Color photographs shot on location at Schaefer's Gardens, Haworth, N.J.

Kneeler photographed at Calvary Church, New York, N.Y. All other interior shots on location at Schaefer's Gardens.

Stained-glass lamp made by Douglas D. Kaiser. Used with permission.

Library of Congress Cataloging-in-Publication Data
Squire, Helen.
    A quilter's garden.

    Bibliography: p.
    1. Quilting—Patterns.   2. Embroidery—Patterns.
3. Decoration and ornament—Plant forms.   I. Title.
TT835.S67   1987   746.46   87-20523
ISBN 0-8007-1558-6

Copyright © 1987 by Helen Squire
Published by the Fleming H. Revell Company
Old Tappan, New Jersey 07675
Printed in the United States of America

TO MY QUILT TEAM—those wonderful friends whose invaluable assistance and encouragement enabled me to write this book. It was a group venture. Each contributed her own special skill: Marian Piehler, *quilting*; Pearl Lucey, *embroidery*; Viola Meese, *research*; Joyce Lockatell, *editorial*.

"Many centuries before written history, gardens of various kinds existed, from the Garden of Eden to the Hanging Gardens of Babylon; the forerunners of modern botanical gardens, these were devoted to ornamental plants, vegetables, culinary herbs, fruit trees, and interesting plants."

Encyclopaedia Britannica, "Botany"

CONTENTS

FOREWORD

"God Almighty first planted a garden," said Francis Bacon. "And, indeed, it is the purest of human pleasures." How many people through the ages could agree with such a simple sentiment? Even those who do not spend time planting and hoeing have known the pleasure of a well-tended garden, a handful of impressive blooms, or an uncultivated field or forest.

For the plants of the Holy Land we have a wonderful source that tells us of the bounty, profusion, symbolism, and practical uses of trees, plants, and flowers that played a part in one culture. Within the Old and New Testaments are descriptions that appeal to the senses and the spirit.

Out of this bountiful blessing has grown A *Quilter's Garden*, a book that combines the delightful flora of the Holy Land with the practical handwork of quilting. The patterns in this volume are especially designed for the beginning or proficient quilter, to be used in a variety of ways. With the finished projects, an individual or group can make useful or decorative pieces for home or church.

What a wonderful way to spend some time. Happy quilting!

THE PUBLISHER

GENERAL
INSTRUCTIONS
ON
QUILTING

How do you plan to quilt a plant?

The twelve plants included in this book were chosen because of their symbolism and pleasing appearance. Their botanical features were carefully researched for authenticity. As quilting patterns, these unusual designs rely on your needle to paint a picture.

These are not chubby hearts to outline quilt around, but simplified designs representing real-life plants, trees, and flowers. To work, they require texture and dimension, created with puffy closeups, flat backgrounds, and smoothly flowing quilted lines. Some embroidery is also necessary to add the details too small to be quilted.

What exactly is quilting?

Quilting is a textile sandwich. The quilt stitch holds the top, the filler (called batting), and the backing fabric together. The quilting design is the pattern the stitches form as they sew through the layers.

Is it difficult to do?

Fig, with its large main leaf and rounded fruit, is the easiest to quilt. Frankincense, with its tiny buds and alternating leaves, is much harder. All designs vary in their degree of difficulty. Beginners will be talked through each step, while advanced quilters can enjoy the challenge of working independently.

RECOMMENDED QUILTING SUPPLIES

Quilting needles: Betweens #8.
Straight pins.
Quilting thread: White, ecru, brown, or
   any accent color.
Quilt batting: Choose from polyester, cot-
   ton, or wool.
Chalk pencil or water-erasable marking
   pen.
Miscellaneous: Pencil, scissors, thimble,
   finger guard.

How do you mark for quilting?

Even though they appear in a dashed form, copy the designs in a continuous solid line. Dashed quilting lines illustrate a sense of airiness, but are not meant to be copied from dash to dash.

Detach the patterns from the book. Tape to a smooth surface—a tabletop or lightbox. Position fabric on top with tape or pins. This prevents it from shifting while copying. Trace the lines showing through the fabric.

For darker, nontransparent fabrics, use cutout shapes of the designs. This is called a silhouette stencil. Place on top of the fabric, copy around its outline.

To mark fabric: Lightly use either a sharp lead pencil, a colored dressmaker's pencil, or a pretested water-erasable pen. Tracings are guidelines. Keep original patterns handy for quick referrals and accurate details.

What does design "flow" mean?

Having the stitches move smoothly from one area to the next is called the flow. When quilting, proceed so that small petals curve and puff, the leaves taper and point, and branches bend as nature intended.

Where do you start quilting?

Quality quilting is made possible by analyzing the flow of the design and placing a strategic stitch where it will do the most good and give maximum movement.

Each pattern has a small star at the best place to begin quilting. Look for it.

Can you quilt without knots?

This is not only possible, but recommended! No unsightly knots should appear in any quilted project! Instead of the difficult method of popping the knot into the batting, try using a long double length of single-strand quilting thread to start. Take one stitch straight through to the backing, then return the needle to the front for the first stitch.

Pull the thread through the batting. Stop midway down the length. Use the first half of the thread to quilt toward yourself. Leave the second half out as a tail to rethread and use later for quilting in the opposite direction.

This eliminates the need for a knot. Both ends quilted away from each other will hold the thread firmly in place.

A longer length of thread divided in half makes for easier handling—more quilting time without tangles and knotting.

What is a thread "tail?"

Quilters call a floating length of quilting thread a tail. There are two kinds. The first refers to a long length left unthreaded until it is needed (see above). The second refers to the short length left in the batting, locked in place, when the quilter scoots off to end.

A short tail can also be used when you run out of thread and want to quilt a small section that does not require a lot of thread.

How is "scooting" done?

Scooting means traveling through the batting when changing places and ending. Two or more needle lengths of thread are caught between the layers of the textile sandwich.

To scoot, finish the last stitch in the area. Continue moving the needle away from that stitch and toward the next area to be quilted. Push the end of the needle along with a thimble, then pivot the needle around and push the point of the needle another length.

Pivot again and again, as needed, to reach the next area. Never let the needle and thread poke through the surface until you are ready to resume quilting or end off. If ending, pull the thread taut on top, clip carefully, and let it release itself into the batting.

Are tiny stitches important?

Tiny stitches come with practice. In good quilting we strive for uniform stitches! The spaces between the stitches should equal their size, on both the top and the bottom of the quilt.

Count stitches by how many appear on the face of the quilt in one inch. Twelve or more stitches to the inch in quiltmaking is unusual but excellent. Five to seven stitches per inch is normal.

To quilt, use your index finger underneath to raise the fabric up slightly in front of the needle, ready for the needle to glide into. Hold the needle in a horizontal position to get even stitches on the bottom. If you come in at your stitches with the needle on the diagonal, a pinprick stitch appears on the wrong side and a regular size on the front.

What quilting method should I use?

Quilting can be done in a hand-held block, in a hoop, or on a frame. The size of your project determines the best method to use.

The purpose is to hold the back fabric taut, let the batting rise toward the top, and lock in this fullness as you quilt. A hoop or an upright frame keeps the backing uniformly rigid and flat. The tighter the back, the fluffier the top appears!

When quilting small projects in which your hand can reach underneath and hold the fabric tight, holding it in your hands gives you the benefit of mobility and the ability to control the amount of fullness in any particular area of the design.

GENERAL
INSTRUCTIONS
ON
EMBROIDERY

Directions

Select designs of your choice. Detach the pages with dashed lines—these are the patterns.

Cut and press necessary fabric ready for marking. For sewing caddy and album cover, mark small individual blocks of fabric. For the church kneeler or wall hanging, mark the entire cloth.

To mark:

(1) Tape pattern to a tabletop or lightbox. This prevents it from shifting while marking.

(2) Position light-colored fabric on top of pattern; tape into place.

(3) Use a light lead pencil to copy design. *Mark in a continuous line, never dashed.* Trace around entire pattern. Untape fabric when finished.

Choose your embroidery-floss colors from suggestions given for each plant.

Use small, four- to six-inch embroidery hoop. Circle should fit over as much of the design as possible. This gives maximum coverage and *keeps the material straight, on grain, and taut.*

RECOMMENDED EMBROIDERY SUPPLIES

Assorted colored floss.
Six-inch or smaller wood embroidery
  hoop.
Assorted embroidery needles.
Thimble, pencil, small scissors.

Embroidering the Names

Use *Pearl's backstitch* to embroider the plant names. It is very legible and very good for detail lettering.

After marking and mounting the fabric in the hoop, work on the top (right) side of fabric. The threaded needle must be placed in the exact hole of the preceding stitch to keep it in a straight line. This prevents it from looking like an outline stitch. Work from left to right, making very small stitches.

Helpful Hints

- Buy and use embroidery needles—their longer length and eyes fit the thread. Use medium- or small-size needles. "Eyes" that are too large will separate the material. A French knot would slip through the hole!

- Use approximately eighteen-inch lengths of thread—longer floss shreds or fuzzes.

- To start, use the smallest knot possible. To end, bring the thread to the back and take two small backstitches into the previously embroidered stitches.

- Trim and clip loose threads and the tails left on the knots. This is especially important when using dark, contrasting colors.

- Press on the wrong side of fabric. Press into a fluffy towel, to raise the embroidered design, ready for quilting.

- Clip and press as you complete each block or design. A little bit of tidiness while working is easier than doing it all later!

Chart of Recommended Embroidery Stitches

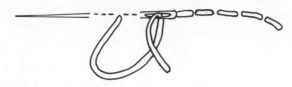

Pearl's Backstitch

Chain Stitch	*Split Stitch*
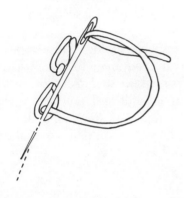	
Satin Stitch	*French Knots*
	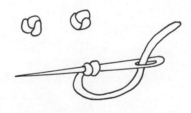
Outline/Stem Stitch	*Straight Stitch*

Church Kneeler

Throughout history, flowers were used as a part of worship. The strewing of blossoms marked festivals to the gods of the ancients. There is a natural, inherent beauty in flowers and fruits of the earth.

What more appropriate use of these twelve quilting designs of the plants of the Holy Land than an embroidered and quilted church kneeler? It is a practical church ornament that quilters can carve with their needles!

MATERIALS NEEDED

Paper or muslin pattern.
Pencil, tape measure, pins, and needles.
Fabric for top and lining. Prequilted print.
Foam cushion, 2″ deep and cut to pew size.
Polyester batting cut 2″ larger than cushion.
Embroidery floss in the colors nature intended.
Hoops. Small embroidery, larger for quilting.
Quilting thread, white or beige. Sewing thread.

Planning the design

To make, simply measure any prayer bench or pew that requires a cushion. Then plan a combination of the patterns and scatter them over the area to be covered.

When designing your own layout, it is not necessary to have quantities of flowers and foliage to provide a garden effect. The placement diagram uses only four patterns: iris, flax, crocus, and anemone. The flax flowers were divided and raised to provide depth and an open place to kneel in.

Marking the fabric

Make a paper or muslin pattern the exact size of the area. To mark light-colored fabrics, tape over the pattern and copy the lines through the fabric. Use a regular lead pencil and mark lightly.

When services follow the seasons of the church year, you may wish to use liturgical colors. To mark these darker fabrics, first trace the designs on cardboard. Cut apart and position on top of fabric. Mark around the silhouette with a white chalk pencil. Refer to your original layout to fill in details.

Embroidering and quilting

Allow for two-inch seam allowance on outside edges. Cut out fabric and place in embroidery hoop. Follow the embroidery suggestions and floss colors listed with each plant. Accent details are necessary for authenticity. Then the whole project should be *outline stitched*.

On dark fabrics, instead of outline embroidering in colors, embroider the entire design in white or gold floss, double strand. This gives a rich, dramatic effect.

To quilt, make a fabric sandwich, with batting between the finished top and lining. Pin and baste together. Outline quilt around the embroidered designs.

Figure 1—Church Kneeler 27½″ x 11½″

Assembling the kneeler

Trim excess batting and lining. Allow regular seam allowance for hand or machine piecing. Use prequilted fabric for side panels and underneath side of cushion.

Place quilted top over foam that has been precut to shape. *Pin wrong sides out.* Tightly pin pieces together around form. A good book on upholstery is helpful here. Leave an opening in back to turn fabrics right side out after sewing. Stuff with foam cushion. Slip stitch opening closed or add a zipper for easier cleaning.

Sewing Caddy

The decorative sewing caddy sits over the armrest of your favorite chair, holding your immediate sewing supplies: scissors, thimble, thread, pins, and needles.

It is an excellent project for beginner quilters who want to try a small quilted sample before they make a wall hanging or quilt. It is also an excellent item to make for fund-raising events!

MATERIALS NEEDED

Fabric (seam allowances are included)
  White: Cut (1) 8" x 18½"
          Cut (2) 7½" x 7½"
          Cut (1) 2½" x 8"
  Print: Cut (1) 7½" x 18"
          Cut (2) 8" x 8"
          Cut (2) 2½" x 7½"
          Cut 70" self bias binding
  Batting: Cut (1) 8" x 18½"
           Cut (2) 8" x 8"
           Cut (1) 2½" x 8"

Thread
  Regular sewing thread: Match color to binding fabric. Embroidery floss: Select accent color for fabric. Quilting thread: Same accent color for pockets, white for diagonal quilted lines.

Miscellaneous supplies
  Quilting and embroidery needles, straight pins, scissors, ruler, marking pen or pencil. Optional: one package single-fold bias tape to match accent color.

To make the pockets

Select two of your favorite designs. Trace the patterns onto the white squares. Follow the embroidery suggestions listed with each pattern. (Anemone is shown here.)

Lay the back fabric face down, then place the batting in the middle and the marked and embroidered block on top. Pin together and baste to prevent shifting.

Follow the suggestions for quilting. Remove basting threads when finished. With sewing thread, attach bias binding to top edge of pocket. Use a running stitch on the top side, then fold over to the back and hem into place. Repeat for second pocket.

To quilt the back and pincushion

Mark a basic one-inch diamond grid on the precut print fabric. Use a light-colored chalk dressmaker's pencil and ruler.

Baste together. The batting and back are slightly larger and should peek out of the sandwich. After quilting and normal shifting, the pattern piece can be trimmed to the correct size.

Quilt all diagonal lines in the same direction. First quilt top right to bottom left, then upper left to bottom right. For this project only, start and end each quilted line with two back stitches in place. The binding will hide them later.

Pincushion instructions

After quilting the top of the cushion (*see above*), pin to the print fabric (2½" x 7½") with

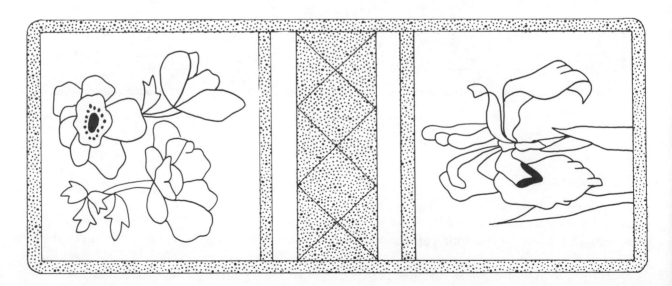

Figure 2—Sewing Caddy 18″ x 7½″

right sides together. Sew the long edges together. Use ¼-inch seam allowance.

Turn right side out and topstitch one short edge closed. Shred loose batting and firmly stuff pincushion. Do not overstuff and distort the shape!

Assembling the sewing caddy

Refer to the placement diagram opposite. Center the pincushion in the middle. On each side leave an equal distance between the cushion and the pockets. Trim any excess batting and fabric. Pin together, then baste around outside edges.

Cut self fabric bias binding or enough purchased single-fold bias tape to go around the entire caddy. Do not start and stop at a corner. Pin into place, ¼-inch from edge. Sew above the crease on the top side. Join tape into loop where it meets. Fold over edge and hem down on underneath side of caddy.

Album Cover

This is a lovely way to showcase your handwork as you try the various quilting designs in the book! The album cover is especially easy to start with, because the real work is done when embroidering the plant. Use the basic *outline stitch*; then follow the outlines later as you quilt. No need to worry about the flow of the design or the size of your quilting stitches in this project!

MATERIALS NEEDED

Photo album 10" x 12"
Fabric
   Lilac solid: Cut (1) 8" x 8" block
             Cut (1) 24" x 14" lining
   Lilac print: Cut (1) 14" x 14" back
             Cut (2) 4" x 14" borders
             (top borders)
             Cut (1) 14" x 4" border
             (side border)
   Purple solid: Cut (2) 11" x 14" linings
   Batting: Cut (1) 24" x 14" batt
Threads
   Purple embroidery floss, purple quilting thread.
   Lilac regular sewing thread.
Miscellaneous supplies
   Quilting and embroidery needle, hoop, straight pins, scissors, marking pen or pencil.

Fabric selection

Myrrh is the featured design in the photograph shown here and on the back of the book in color. Lilac and purple fabrics were used for the sample, so these are the colors referred to in the directions. Please experiment with various color selections as well as with the designs you choose. Look at each plant's description and floss colors for appropriate ideas.

Since the borders are to be mitered, limit your selections to all-over prints that match easily.

Embroidery and quilting

Place the lilac square over the pattern, tape in place, and trace. Do not copy the seven-inch

quilting box now. Embroider any detail embellishments; then follow the pencil line to embroider the entire outline. Use a small hoop.

When finished, press block face down into a fluffy towel. This raises the stitches, ready for quilting.

Lay the lilac lining and batting together. Position the block to the right of center. Pin three inches down from top and three inches in from the right side. Baste to prevent shifting.

Follow the quilting directions provided for each design, but quilt on the outside of the embroidered stitches. Since the album cover is a small project, just hold the backing fabric taut as you quilt.

Attaching the borders

After quilting, measure and mark a seven-inch box around the design. This becomes the guideline for sewing straight borders. Lay the precut strips of print fabric facedown on top of the quilted block. Overlap fabric widths at corners.

Allowing ¼-inch seams, pin the top piece first. Use quilting thread to sew through the four layers of print, solid, batt, and lining. Repeat for the right side and bottom pieces.

The left side is done the same way, using the fourteen-inch square print. This piece includes the border width and enough fabric for the back of the album, plus seam allowances.

How to miter

The secret to a successful miter is to start and stop a few stitches from the edges of the box! This gives you leeway in forming a perfect corner.

Finger press borders flat, with face side up. From the top put a pin through the borders exactly at the corner. Turn under overlapped widths to create a diagonal line, called a miter. Repin to hold in place. Repeat for all four corners.

Finger crease, then sew corners together with a slip stitch or hemstitch. Sew with lilac thread, single strand. Lift away from batting and trim to ¼-inch seams.

Finishing the album cover

Wrap the cover around the album to get an actual fit. Allow extra room for opening a spiral

binding. Mark along the outer edges with a water-erasable pen.

Join the purple lining to the short sides of the cover. Position and pin with right sides together. Adjust seam allowances as necessary to fit your individual album's size.

Stitch together, following marked guidelines. Stop and end at the top and bottom edges, to permit easier turning under of the seams. Trim seam allowances. Wrap the album with the cover, pinning tightly along the edges until the lining fits snugly. Be neat inside.

Slip stitch along the edges. Hide knots and end off by backstitching, then scooting into the batting. When the cover becomes soiled, remove the stitches and launder, then slipstitch back in place. (See Figure 3, p. 80.)

Wall Hanging

A quilted panel representing the plants of the Holy Land seems a logical choice for use as a decorative wall hanging in any Sunday school or church building. Where services follow a liturgical church year, you may wish to use symbolic colors in vestments and hangings: white, red, green, and violet.

Of all the colors that mark the events of Jesus' life and ministry, white or green seem the most practical background for use in this project. The purity and joy of white is universal, and green symbolizes nature's color, hope, and immortality. To use the others would be inappropriate.

After choosing the color, next decide on the type of fabric to be quilted. Consider carefully if the finished wall hanging will be washed or dry-cleaned later. Sometimes, if they hang in a church, quilts are only vacuumed!

MATERIALS NEEDED

Fabrics
   Solid fabric: 1⅔ yards (44/45″ wide)
   Solid backing fabric: 1⅔ yards
Batting
   (1) crib-size batt (45″ x 60″) Mountain Mist® polyester batting
Miscellaneous
   Brown quilting thread, brown embroidery floss, needles, straight pins, scissors, marking pencil, Chakoner®, water-erasable pen, yardstick, white thread for basting.

Tone-on-tone quilting explained

In patchwork and appliqué quilts, color and shapes draw the viewer's eye. In whitework quilting, only the stitches and the designs they form can catch and hold the eye. White fabric quilted with white thread is the purest form of historical quilting. Nowadays, quilters use off-white (ecru) thread on beige, rose on pink, or any tonal combination.

Making a full-size pattern

In "Project Worksheets and Patterns" find the pattern for the Everlasting Chain design used in this wall hanging. Detach or copy onto tracing paper all the patterns in the book, both for the plants (twelve) and the chain (three).

On a separate piece of paper, 45″ x 58″, reassemble and trace the complete layout of the patterns. Refer to the worksheet on p. 81. **Hint:** Instead of taping paper together to make a pattern large enough, try using an old sheet or some inexpensive muslin. It is an easier way to plan a quilt. Use a water-erasable pen to mark, and wipe off any mistakes with water! When the layout and measurements are perfect, use a permanent, indelible pen to darken the lines.

Marking the quilt top

Tape the full pattern to a smooth surface. Iron the top fabric, then position it over the pattern. Pin in place to prevent shifting. Use a yardstick and a Chakoner® to mark the lines straight. The Chakoner® is a plastic heart that contains powdered chalk for drawing a fine line. Most quilt shops sell it. Trace the rest of the designs with a dressmaker's chalk pencil or a regular sharp lead pencil. Copy with a solid line. A dashed line is only used to illustrate quilting patterns.

A water-erasable marking pen is *not* recommended for this project, as it might evaporate before you finish embroidering and quilting.

Embroidering the names

Every plant chapter has a full-size drawing of the plant's name, as well as the actual embroidered name in a reduced version.

The wall hanging was designed for the names but was photographed without them. Position the correct names in the open spaces beneath the blocks. Mark for embroidery. Use a hoop and *Pearl's backstitch* (described on p. 18 of the "General Instructions on Embroidery").

Closely follow the other suggestions listed in each chapter for embroidering authentic details. When this is completed, press the top face down into a fluffy towel.

(*Continue on page 28.*)

Basting the layers together

Make a textile sandwich of the backing, the polyester batting, and the prepressed embroidered top. Pin baste around the blocks and along the Everlasting Chain. Keep the back fabric taut!

Use white basting thread to take large, loose stitches radiating out from the center toward the edges. First baste in the north, south, east, and west directions, then diagonally into the four corners. Keep all knots on the top for easier removal later.

To quilt: Follow the directions given for each plant. Use brown quilting thread for a stronger visual impact!

Quilting on the frame

Whenever your hands cannot reach underneath the quilt project to feel the needle poking through from the top, you need to use a frame! An oval hoop, 18″ x 27″ is an inexpensive investment in quilting supplies. It covers an area large enough to quilt without constantly having to move it around.

Frames are available in all sizes and prices—from flat boards with C clamps to the traditional upright frame with ratchets for tightening.

Quilting is often done by groups of women working together—an occasion called a "quilting bee," which also serves as an opportunity for socializing. (Read more about group quilting on p. 93).

Finishing off the edges

The flora designs, the interlocking borders, and the embroidered names of the plants provide enough interest in this wall hanging. To add further details often leads to an effect of fussiness.

It is therefore recommended that you use a basic method of finishing to bind off the edges. Choose one of the twelve different sewing techniques in the back of this book (*see* p. 89).

Displaying the Plants of the Holy Land Quilt

To hang the wall quilt, attach a muslin "sleeve" along the top edge of the back. Cut a strip of fabric six inches high by the width of the quilt. Turn raw edges under, with a ½-inch seam allowance.

Appliqué the sleeve into place. Be careful that the stitches only catch the backing and do not show on the top of the quilt.

Insert a wooden or metal rod through the opening. To hang, fancy finials can be rested on wall brackets, or else attach a thin wire to a hidden piece of wood in the sleeve. Small drapery weights, tacked to the bottom corners of the back, help to keep it hanging straight.

PLANTS
OF
THE
HOLY LAND

Almond

"I have come down among the almond trees to see the young plants in the valley, to see the new leaves on the vines and the blossoms on the pomegranate trees."

Song of Solomon 6:11 TEV

Latin

Almond—*Amygolalus communis,* also called *Prunus amygdalus* and *Prunus communis.*

Description

A small tree that grows ten to twenty-five feet tall, the almond is the most beautiful of the fruit trees when in bloom! Its large, pale flowers, pink to white in color, are the first to blossom in spring. After flowering, oblong elliptical leaves appear on short spurs.

If peach trees, its kissing cousins, are planted nearby, the almond will set more fruit. Initially the almond's fuzzy young fruit grows to resemble the closely related peach, but instead of becoming plump with flesh, develops hard green husks. When ripe, the outer cover splits open, curls outward, and discharges a shell. This soft inner brown covering protects the one-inch, oval nut, seen after shelling.

There are two types of almonds grown: "sweet," with pink flowers and edible nuts, and "bitter," with white flowers and nuts that cannot be eaten until processed.

General Information

Palestine, Syria, and other countries of the Near East cultivated the almond tree. As with any delicacy or rare spice, the Holy Land peoples prized the almond as a gift of commerce. Genesis 43:11 (KJV), mentioned the almond nut as a suitable gift: ". . . take of the best fruits in the land in your vessels, and carry down the man a present, a little balm, and a little honey, spices, and myrrh, nuts, and almonds."

The identification of the almond tree in the Bible is certain. Its most apparent characteristic, early blossoms, were mentioned often (Song of Solomon 6:11).

Numbers 17:8 (KJV) describes Aaron's staff as blooming in the tent of the tabernacle; it ". . . was budded, and brought forth buds, and bloomed blossoms, and yielded almonds."

The almond tree has always been valued, not only for its beauty (Exodus 25:33, 34) but also for its fruit. Consumed as nuts, oil of almond, and almond milk, it has been an essential household item for centuries.

Embroidery Suggestions

Two ideas are incorporated into the almond design: the early spring blossom and the fruit-laden branch in fall.

Use either a *split stitch* or *straight stitch* to represent the stamens. Each attaches at its base to the flower, with an anther for catching pollen at its tip. Attach a *French knot* to the free end, then add a few more knots inside the blossom.

The prominent center vein of the leaf has been embroidered with the *outline stitch*. This stitch also illustrates an unfurled leaf at the top. *Do not quilt* along these lines later, as it would flatten the design.

The *satin stitch* gives texture to the peachlike husks.

For maximum effect the entire design can be outline embroidered in nature's colors, or you may use brown floss throughout.

Floss colors: Pink or white for the flower. Green leaves and brown for the branch and stems. The oval husks are green. The brown inner shell and nut are not shown.

Refer to the "General Instructions on Embroidery" (p. 17) for how-to directions, supplies, and a chart of recommended stitches.

Quilting Suggestions

To start in the center of the block, place your threaded needle at the star. With half the thread, quilt down the right side of the three-pronged group of leaves into the branch, scooting off to end your thread. Use the second half of your original thread to finish the first leaf. Next quilt the almond nuts on either side. Take one stitch at a time, to get the flowing oval shape.

Quilting outward from the center, finish quilting the rest of the leaves and fruit. Quilt the flowers separately, one petal at a time. Do not quilt the embroidered stamens. If French knots have not been added, then a few random stitches are necessary to hold down the fullness in the center area.

The techniques of quilting, that is, no knots, scooting, and tails, are explained in the "General Instructions on Quilting" (p. 13).

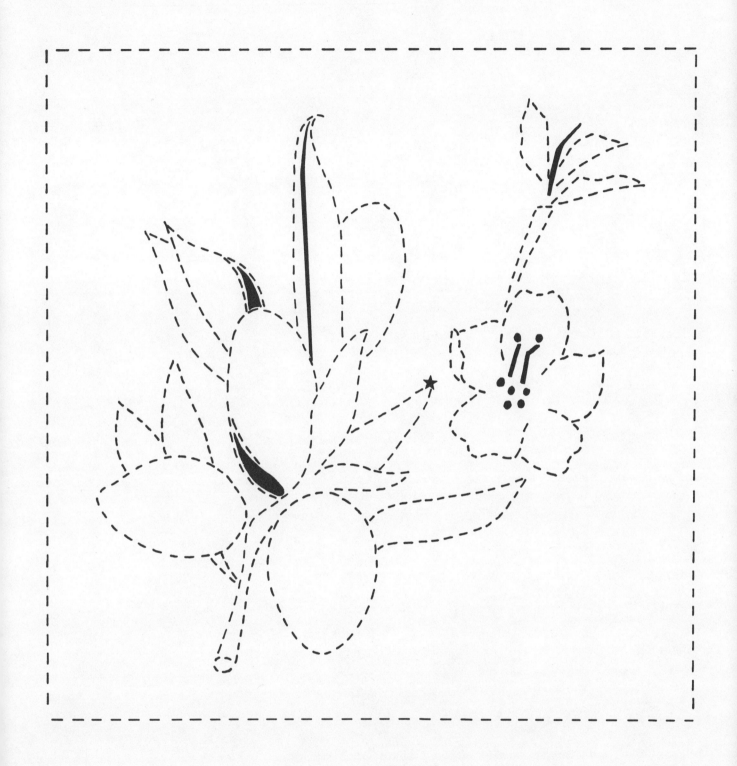

Almond

DETACH PAGE FROM BOOK

For light-colored fabrics—Position pattern under fabric and copy the design in a continuous line.

For darker fabrics—Make a silhouette stencil by copying the pattern on cardboard and cutting out the shape. Position stencil on top of fabric and mark around the designs.

Anemone

"And why take ye thought for raiment? Consider the lilies of the field, how they grow; they toil not, neither do they spin: And yet I say unto you, That even Solomon in all his glory was not arrayed like one of these."

Matthew 6:28, 29 KJV

Latin

Anemone—*Anemone coranana*. The poppy anemone of the buttercup family *Ranunculaceae*.

Description

A showy flower with an unusual depth and intensity of color and many varieties, the poppy anemone also ranges from six to twelve inches high. Like most wind-pollinated plants, the petals are insignificant or missing altogether (in such cases the sepals appear petallike).

Numerous and striking stamens surround a deep blue-black center. The fruit consists of several, small dry seeds.

On the stems, the characteristic ruff of foliage just below the blossoms is not really leaves, but a whorl of three leaflike bracts. Anemones are also unusual in that they continue to grow after they have been picked, because they have a meristem, a region of active growth at this "collar of leaves."

The cup-shaped blossoms come in shades of white, pink, rose, red, blue, and purple. (The violet and indigo are spectacular!) Anemones bloom in almost every color but yellow, which seems curious, considering their close relationship to buttercups.

General Information

These exotic-looking plants grow wild in the Middle East. A small flower, with large, poppylike blossoms, anemones grow abundantly throughout Palestine.

The Greeks called the flower, *krinon*, meaning "wind." Sometimes the plant is called "windflowers" and sometimes it is called "lily."

Scholars do not agree as to the exact translation of the Hebrew word *shoshan*, which appears in the Scriptures as: "lily of the valleys" (Song of Solomon 2:1, 2), "among the lilies" (Song of Solomon 2:16), and "lips like lilies" (Song of Solomon 5:13).

A number of bulb flowers have been suggested for this lily: crocus, Easter lily, anemone, narcissus, iris, and tulip. The primary clue as to the particular flower meant seems to lie in the content of each passage.

With their brilliant colors and unlimited shades, it is not difficult to envision Jesus speaking of the anemone, when He compared King Solomon to the "lilies of the field," in Matthew 6:28, 29.

Embroidery Suggestions

Having three flowers in one quilting design is a lot! You do not need to add extra emphasis with too much embroidery. This would be really "gilding the lily."

A circlet of *French knots* surrounding the *satin stitch* on the full-view flower will suffice. Whenever you use the basic *outline stitch* to embroider everything, it enhances the design and gives you a chance to use more colors!

Floss colors: White or any brilliant shade of pink, red, violet, blue, or purple for the petallike sepals. Green for the stems and foliage. Black or dark blue for the French knots and center. Otherwise use brown floss, double strand, throughout.

Refer to the "General Instructions on Embroidery" (p. 17) for a hint on the proper size needle to use.

Quilting Suggestions

Scoot through the batting and bring your needle up at the star. Quilt completely around the center's outline; then scoot through the batting to the first petal shape.

Quilt with small stitches. To lock in as much fullness as possible, remember to keep the back fabric taut.

After finishing the first flower, quilt outward from the center area. Keep turning your block, if hand held, so that your quilting stitches always come toward you.

Quilt stems, leaflets, and each blossom, curve by curve. Refer to the "General Instructions on Quilting" (p. 13) for more suggested quilting techniques.

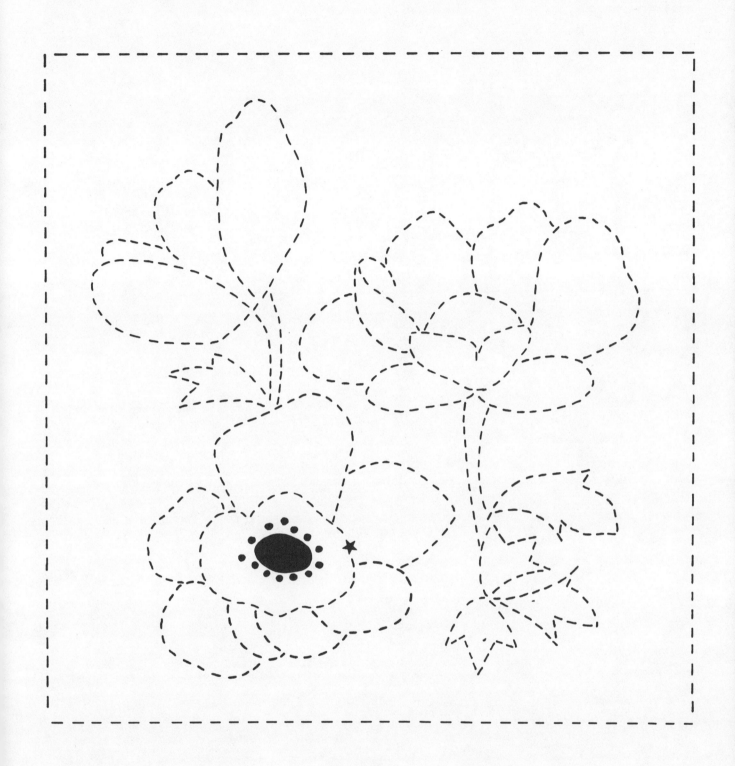

Anemone

DETACH PAGE FROM BOOK

For light-colored fabrics—Position pattern under fabric and copy the design in a continuous line.

For darker fabrics—Make a silhouette stencil by copying the pattern on cardboard and cutting out the shape. Position stencil on top of fabric and mark around the designs.

Apricot

"*As the apple tree among the trees of the wood, so is my beloved among the sons. I sat down under his shadow with great delight, and his fruit was sweet to my taste.*"

Song of Solomon, 2:3 KJV

Latin

Apricot—*Prunus armeniaca*. Stone fruit of the family *Rosaceae*.

Description

A good shade tree, the apricot grows twenty feet tall and has branches that spread twenty-five to thirty feet and are completely covered with dense foliage. Early spring brings a profusion of white or pink cupped blossoms, with five petals, borne singly or doubly at a node, on very short stems. Later, its broad, dark green leaves are held erect on the twigs of the knobby limbs. In summer, a golden yellow fruit grows where the flowers bloomed.

The round fruit (*not shown*) is smooth, very aromatic, and has a taste somewhere between that of a peach and a plum. Its sweetness not only refreshes but revitalizes.

General Information

Native to China, the apricot is cultivated in Southeast Asia, North Africa, Iran, and Syria. While it is a common fruit tree, no clear evidence exists of its growing in Palestine during biblical times.

However, scholars do suggest that perhaps the word *apple*, enumerated with the other chief trees (Joel 1:12), meant *apricot*. The apricot's description does seem to fit the concept, while the Hebrew *tappuah*, of ancient times, referred to a hard, bitter fruit, more like a crab apple.

Conceivably the "apples of gold" (Proverbs 25:11) could be golden colored apricots! Somehow the "apple of his eye," mentioned in Deuteronomy 32:10 and Zechariah 2:8, would lose something in the translation if we called it "the apricot of his eye"!

Embroidery Suggestions

There is a certain amount of embroidery necessary to give authenticity to the apricot quilting design.

Use either a *split stitch* or *straight stitch* to represent the stamens. The stamen (or filament) is attached at its base to the flower and has an anther for catching pollen at its free end.

Attach a *French knot* at the tip of each anther, then add more French knots. Refer to the solid dark lines and dots.

The *satin stitch* gives depth to the nodes along the branches.

Floss colors: White, light pink, or dark pink for the blossoms; gold or yellow for the stamens and anthers; brown branches; and dark green leaves. Or the entire design can be *outline stitched* in dark brown floss, double strand.

Refer to the "General Instructions on Embroidery" (p. 17) for how-to directions, supplies, and a chart of recommended stitches.

Quilting Suggestions

At the star, start with a double tail of thread and continue quilting around the entire leaf first. Scoot under the petals of the large flower. Then scoot over to the vein and quilt down the vein, stem, and the branch. This will keep the back fabric tight, while locking in the correct fullness on the top fabric, necessary for the flower and background leaf.

Quilt petal by petal, skipping under the embroidered stamens and any French knots. If you do not choose to embroider the knots, a few random quilting stitches are needed in the center of the flowers in order to hold down the fullness. The petals should cup around the center.

The curvy lines of the apricot design only permit one small stitch at a time, but you'll consider the time well spent when you see the petals and leaves curl up!

Quilt the branch and buds on the left-hand top section last.

Quilters who already quilt ten to twelve stitches to the inch do not have to read the "General Instructions on Quilting" or the helpful hints for getting the maximum effect from the quilting design. Everything they quilt looks terrific!

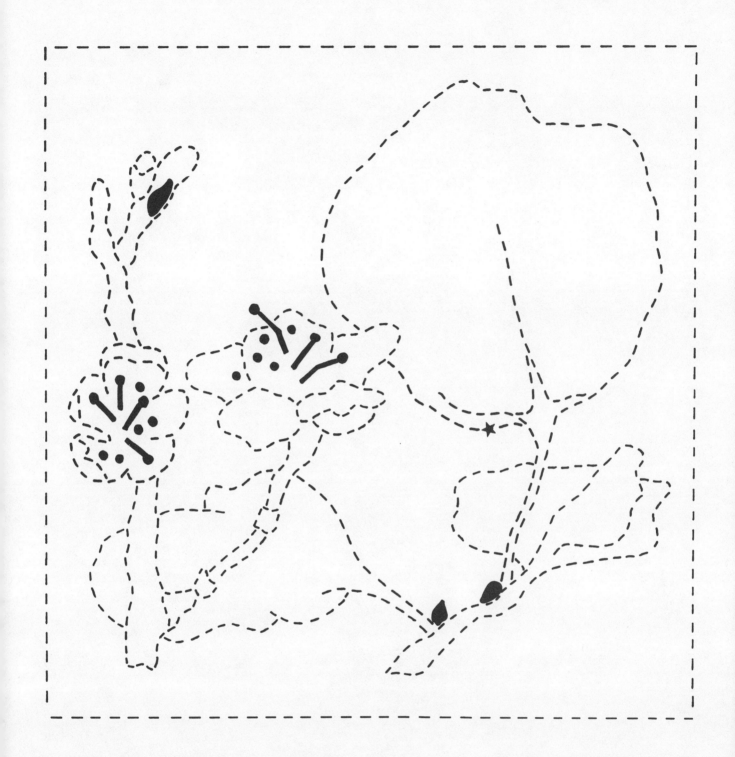

Apricot

DETACH PAGE FROM BOOK

For light-colored fabrics—Position pattern under fabric and copy the design in a continuous line.

For darker fabrics—Make a silhouette stencil by copying the pattern on cardboard and cutting out the shape. Position stencil on top of fabric and mark around the designs.

Crocus

"You are like a lovely orchard bearing precious fruit, with the rarest of perfumes; nard and saffron, calamus and cinnamon, and perfume from every other incense tree, as well as myrrh and aloes, and every other lovely spice."

Song of Solomon 4:13, 14 TLB

Latin

Crocus—*Crocus sativus.* A member of the iris family, *Iridaceae.*

Description

It is easy to recognize these small, bulbous plants. Crocuses have grassy leaves and short stems that bear one solitary, elongated flower. A low-growing herb, its cuplike blossoms bloom abundantly in shades of purple, lavender, white, and yellow.

The stigmas of the flowers are narrow, threadlike, and a vivid orange color.

General Information

These small flowers originated in Asia Minor and grow wild in the Mediterranean region. Evidence exists that *Crocus sativus* was cultivated in Palestine for its yield of saffron. King Solomon compared his bride to a garden planted with saffron and other fragrant spices and trees (Song of Solomon 4:14). Ancient people used the aromatic petals to perfume banquet halls and guests' clothing.

"Meadow saffron" (*Colchicum*), also called autumn crocus, is grown and harvested for its stigmas. These are picked out from the centers of the flowers and dried. They can be ground, used in whole strands or pressed cakes. It would take fields of flowers to provide enough golden saffron for spicing. Almost four thousand stigmas are used to make one ounce, and over sixty thousand are needed to make one pound of saffron!

The expensive saffron is valued for both its flavoring and coloring properties. Once used for dyeing textiles, now we know it better as a yellow vegetable dye, useful to color butter, cheese, and confections. It is also used in medicine.

Scholars know the crocus by the Greek and Arabic name *krokos* and the Hebrew name, *karkōm* (Isaiah 35:1; Song of Solomon 2:1).

Embroidery Suggestions

Refer to the darker lines for the minimum amount of embroidery necessary to enhance the crocus quilting design.

Use an *outline stitch* along the grasslike leaves appearing with the flowers. Stitch one or two leaves on the main plant and along the small bud.

For the important, feathery stigmas of the crocus, choose either the *satin stitch* or the lighter looking *chain stitch*.

To better emphasize the entire design, trace the pattern onto your fabric and embroider everything with the *outline stitch*.

Floss colors: Embroider the stems and leaves in green and the stigmas in gold or orange. The flowers can be white, cream, lavender, lilac, purple, or yellow. Use a double strand of floss. You can also use brown floss to outline the entire design.

Refer to the "General Instructions on Embroidery" (p. 17), for how-to directions, supplies, and a chart of recommended stitches.

Quilting Suggestions

At the star, start with a long "tail" or double length of thread. This is the best place to begin quilting. Use one-half of the thread length to quilt down the crocus petal, into the stem, and around the base. Any extra thread can be used on the first grasslike leaf, to the right of the flower.

Thread your needle again and use the second half of the thread to quilt in the opposite direction, around the remaining petals and sepals. Remember to let the stigmas fall free over the petals. *Do not quilt across them.*

Quilt in a flowing line around the flowers and down the leaves. If you have used outline embroidery, then only quilt along one side of the stitches. This raises them slightly, while quilting both sides causes them to flatten.

Refer to the "General Instructions on Quilting" (p. 13) for additional information on "where and why" we quilt.

Crocus

DETACH PAGE FROM BOOK

For light-colored fabrics—Position pattern under fabric and copy the design in a continuous line.

For darker fabrics—Make a silhouette stencil by copying the pattern on cardboard and cutting out the shape. Position stencil on top of fabric and mark around the designs.

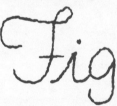

"And he shall judge among many people, and rebuke strong nations afar off; and they shall beat their swords into plowshares, and their spears into pruninghooks: nation shall not lift up a sword against nation, neither shall they learn war anymore. But they shall sit every man under his vine and under his fig tree; and none shall make them afraid: for the mouth of the Lord of hosts hath spoken it."

Micah 4:3, 4 KJV

Latin

Fig—*Ficus carica*. A member of the mulberry family, *Moraceae*. The flowering plant order *Urticales*.

Description

Fig trees may grow ten to twenty-five feet tall and spread to an equal or greater distance. Large leaves and thick foliage make the fig an ideal shade tree. The trunk and branches, covered with pearl-gray bark, are curved and irregular, which gives older trees an attractive gnarled shape.

The inconspicuous, greenish colored flowers lack petals. Tiny figs begin to develop at the juncture of the old wood and the new buds.

What we see as the "fig fruit" is really the stem tip—a fleshy, pearlike receptacle called syconium. The inner walls are the true fruit. However, it is all edible and delicately sweet! Oblong figs grow one to three inches and are mostly white, brown, or purplish in color when ripe. They have a characteristic scar on the broad end of the stem.

Between figs and fig wasps, there exists a symbiotic relationship. The wasp pollinates the fig, which in return provides specialized flowers required by the wasp for its reproductive requirements. *This growth appears two or three times a year!*

General Information

One of the first of the fruits mentioned in the Bible (Genesis 3:7), the fig tree bears fruit for fifty years or more and yields almost fifty pounds annually. This popular and bountiful tree provides a double or even triple yearly crop. Scripture well documents its unusual growing habit. Obviously a valuable tree of commerce, it is also a favorite shade tree of the Middle East.

The prophet Micah speaks of every man sitting contentedly "under his vine and under his fig tree" (Micah 4:4), and Isaiah 36:16 and Zechariah 3:10 use the fig as a symbol of safety and prosperity.

The threesome of fig, vine, and pomegranate made up a major fruit crop of the Holy Land (Numbers 13:23). The use of the esteemed fig in medicine as a poultice is referred to twice: once in 1 Kings 20:7 and again in Isaiah 38:21. In all, the Bible mentions the fig more than fifty times!

Embroidery Suggestions

The fig's large leaves are easily recognizable in art motifs. The apron of clothing referred to in Genesis 3:7 was made of the leaf, the most prominent part of this quilting design.

To accent the shape of the leaf, an *outline stitch* is used along the main veins. Quilting emphasizes the rest.

To enhance the entire design, continue to outline embroider all the parts. Use colors of the authentic tree or use brown floss, double strand, throughout.

Floss colors: dark green for the leaves, brown for the branches, and your choice of white, brown, or purple for the ripening figs.

Refer to the "General Instructions on Embroidery" (p. 17) for how-to directions, supplies, and a chart of recommended stitches.

Quilting Suggestions

Start with a double length of quilting thread at the star. Quilt down and around the tip, counterclockwise. It is not necessary to quilt along the veins if you have embroidered them first! If you omitted embroidery, then follow the dark lines for quilting.

Next, scoot over and quilt the tree branch. Down one side, keeping the back taut, then down the other side. It is always best to quilt parallel lines in the same direction.

Quilt the figs in a flowing, smooth line. Try your smallest quilting, one stitch at a time, to give it the maximum curve.

The more you quilt, the flatter the design. The less you quilt, the fluffier! The quilted veins in the smaller leaf will flatten it, while not quilting the veins in the larger leaf will permit it greater fullness. This gives more dimension to the block. Read the "General Instructions on Quilting" (p. 13) for more details on how this theory works.

Fig

DETACH PAGE FROM BOOK

For light-colored fabrics—Position pattern under fabric and copy the design in a continuous line.

For darker fabrics—Make a silhouette stencil by copying the pattern on cardboard and cutting out the shape. Position stencil on top of fabric and mark around the designs.

"Who can find a virtuous woman? for her price is far above rubies. The heart of her husband doth safely trust in her, so that he shall have no need of spoil. She will do him good and not evil all the days of her life. She seeketh wool, and flax, and worketh willingly with her hands. . . . She maketh fine linen, and selleth it; and delivereth girdles unto the merchant."

Proverbs 31:10–13, 24 KJV

Latin

Flax—*Linum usitatissimum*. A plant and its fiber, of the family *Linaceae*.

Description

Flax flowers have five petals and are usually blue, sometimes whitish in color. Narrow leaves grow alternately on the stalk.

This is a tender annual plant, with small globular bolls that contain the seeds.

When densely planted for fiber, plants average three to four feet in height, slender stalks and branches becoming concentrated at the top. Plants cultivated for seed are shorter, having many branches.

General Information

Flax, one of the oldest textile fibers, and evidence of fine linen fabrics made from it have been discovered in ancient Egyptian tombs. Valued for its strength and durability, the smooth surface of the linen repels soil. Stronger than cotton, it dries more quickly, is more slowly affected by exposure to sunlight, and can be bleached to a pure white. Because linen carries heat away from the body, garments made from it have a cooling effect on the wearer.

References to flax's growth, harvesting, and end uses appear often in the Scriptures:

In linen making the flax is dried (Joshua 2:6), deseeded, then retted and dried again. The fibers are separated from the inner core by hackling, then combed in preparation for spinning into thread and weaving into cloth. The short, tangled fibers that are left over from the combing are the "tow" referred to in Judges 15:14; 16:9; and Isaiah 1:31. Tow makes a coarse yarn, which was used for oil lamp wicks (Isaiah 42:3).

Modern uses of flax for twine or rope and flaxseeds for linseed oil and cattle fodder were not known in biblical times. Flax fibers are now used for products requiring strength and the ability to withstand moisture, such as canvas, fire hose, and fishnets.

Embroidery Suggestions

The minimum amount of embroidery necessary to enhance the flax quilting design is:

A *straight stitch* for the stamen, and a double *overcast stitch* at the tips. Emphasize the stringy look of the main flower with an *outline stitch*.

For maximum effect, the entire design can be traced onto your fabric block and embroidered in an outline stitch. Floss colors: blue for flowers, green for leaves, and so on, would be appropriate, or the whole design can be embroidered in brown floss, double strand.

Refer to the "General Instructions on Embroidery" (p. 17), for how-to directions, needed supplies, and a chart of recommended stitches.

Quilting Suggestions

Look for the small, printed star for the best place to begin. Start on the middle stem in the block, then follow around each leaf, alternating on the stalk. Next quilt the flowers, petal by petal. Continue outward until the last, small bud on the left side is finished. Then quilt outwards from the center, toward the right side.

Embroidery is shown in solid lines on all the patterns. But, be careful, not all lines are meant to be quilted! To quilt the stamens here would flatten the effect created by the quilted petals.

Select your method of quilting after reading the "General Instructions on Quilting" (p. 13). This design is slightly more difficult than the others, when making hand-held blocks the size of the sewing caddy or album cover. This is because all those stitches along the narrow vertical lines of the stems and leaves distort the grain of the fabric. Therefore, the fingers underneath have to be very busy keeping the back fabric taut. Meanwhile, on the top, your thumb should be pushing and rolling ever so slightly the necessary fabric to be locked into the leaf, while smoothing flat any extra fabric that is threatening to puff up in between the leaves and flowers.

If you use a frame, the regular quilting of the vertical lines should be no problem, since the whole cloth of the quilt, top and back, is uniformly held taut.

Flax

DETACH PAGE FROM BOOK

For light-colored fabrics—Position pattern under fabric and copy the design in a continuous line.

For darker fabrics—Make a silhouette stencil by copying the pattern on cardboard and cutting out the shape. Position stencil on top of fabric and mark around the designs.

Frankincense

"And the LORD said unto Moses, Take unto thee sweet spices, stacte, and onycha, and galbanum; these sweet spices with pure frankincense: of each shall there be a like weight. And thou shalt make it a perfume, a confection after the art of the apothecary, tempered together, pure and holy."

Exodus 30:34, 35 KJV

Latin

Frankincense—*Boswellia Carteri.*

Description

Frankincense is the gum resin obtained from the low-growing species of the *Boswellia* tree or shrub. Its small, white, five-petaled flowers grow in tight clusters on long flower spikes. They are almost hidden among the pinnate leaves, on their erect, branching stems.

Both branches and trunk exude a gum in the form of glittering drops. When the bark is peeled back or incisions are made in it, a resinous sap forms—a milky colored juice that becomes hardened on exposure to the air and forms one-inch oblong globules or lumps called tears.

This fragrant resin from the tree is frankincense. Used alone or with other materials, it is the chief ingredient of incense. When heated or burned, the drops give off a strong balsam odor.

General Information

From earliest times, southern Arabia had been a trading center for fragrant spices, resins, and gums. These dried parts of plants were cultivated for their aromatic and desirable substances. Priests employed them in worship, incantations, and rituals.

The native Palestinian "frankincense tree" (*see* Song of Solomon 4:6) was an important ceremonial plant, its gum used for sacrificial services (Leviticus 2:15, 16; 24:7). It makes an incense that burns freely (hence its name, *frank-incense*, or "free burning") and spreads a very pungent perfume.

The limited supply of the incense made it very costly and a lucrative item for the extensive and profitable spice trade of biblical times. King Solomon received part of his huge income from the "traffick of the spice merchants" (1 Kings 10:15 KJV).

One of the most highly valued of all ancient incense gums, frankincense was an ingredient in the holy anointing oil used only in Israel's tabernacle (Exodus 30:34). While all gifts of "gold and incense" (Isaiah 60:6) were valuable, the presentation of frankincense in Matthew 2:11, to the infant Jesus, had a special significance.

Embroidery Suggestions

One detail is needed to complete the frankincense design. To show depth in the tiny buds and blossoms hidden among the leaves, use two small *straight stitches*. Inside of each point of the open blossoms, take two parallel stitches. Use a double strand of embroidery floss and do not quilt these lines later.

The entire design can be embroidered in an *outline stitch*, using a variety of colorful floss or brown floss throughout. This would give the maximum effect. *See* "General Instructions on Embroidery" (p. 19), for a chart of recommended stitches, how-to directions, and supplies.

Floss colors: white or greenish white flowers, pink lines, green leaves and stems, and a brown branch. The resin gum is not shown in the design.

Quilting Suggestions

Unlike quilting easy designs, such as nice, fat, mushy hearts—where the basic shape is everything—trying to quilt flowering plants is much harder!

It is like painting a picture with your needle. By controlling air pockets of space, you create the foreground, background, details, and texture.

Start at the printed star. Use a double tail, with the shorter length left free. Begin quilting with the longer thread down the entire stem into the branch. Quilt around the base and up the opposite side, continue into the first burst of flowers.

Take small stitches in order to be able to get points along the sides of the starlike flowers. The buds will have to be quilted in a figure-eight motif. Strive for flowing movement and to lock in as much fullness as you can.

Use your second half of the tail to quilt the top leaf, then each of the featherlike leaves.

Scoot in and start again, without a tail, for the leaves in the foreground. Keep the back fabric taut and let these leaves really stand out, to show perspective.

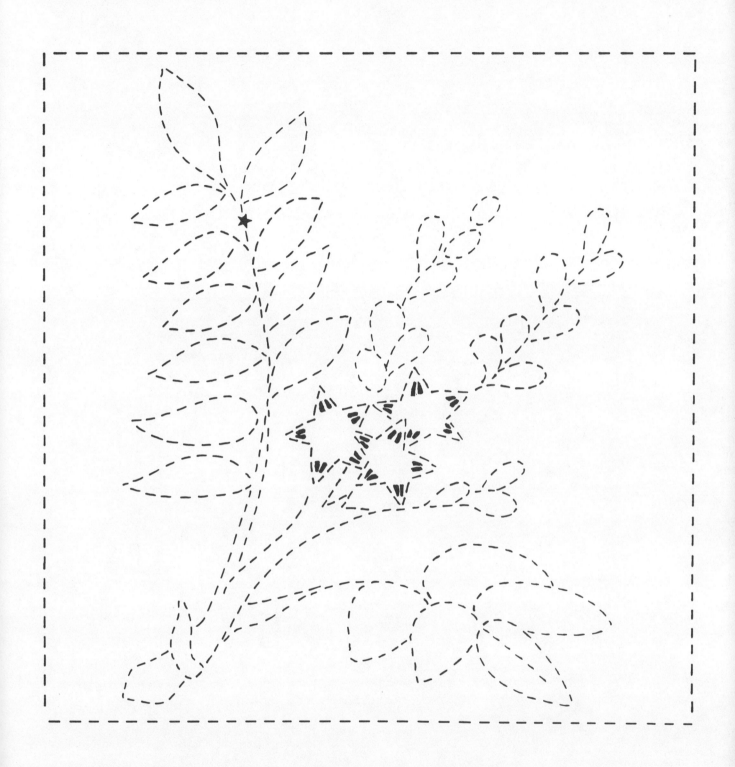

Frankincense

DETACH PAGE FROM BOOK

For light-colored fabrics—Position pattern under fabric and copy the design in a continuous line.

For darker fabrics—Make a silhouette stencil by copying the pattern on cardboard and cutting out the shape. Position stencil on top of fabric and mark around the designs.

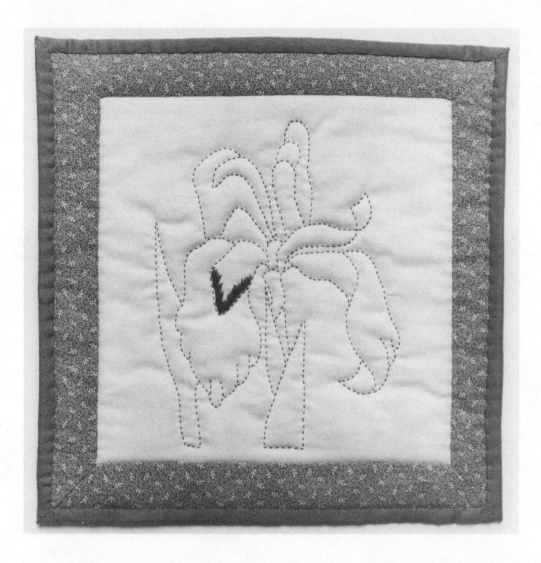

Iris

"*I will be as the dew unto Israel: he shall grow as the lily, and cast forth his roots as Lebanon. His branches shall spread, and his beauty shall be as the olive tree, and his smell as Lebanon.*"

Hosea 14:5, 6 KJV

Latin

Iris—*Iridaceae pseudacorus.*

Description

Bearded or beardless irises can be either bulbous or rhizomic and grow to a height of three to forty inches or more.

The yellow flag iris (*I. pseudacorus*), shown, a direct descendant of the original wild species, grows from thick underground stems, called rhizomes or roots. It bears bright, two-inch flowers and grows best in wet places. With other types of irises it shares the characteristics of sword-shaped leaves and a distinctive flower structure. All irises have six petallike floral segments, the more erect inner ones (petals), called standards, and the usually drooping outer ones (sepals), called falls.

Bearded irises have a fuzzy, bright-colored strip at the top of the fall. The yellow flag iris has a darker area of brown veins in the same place.

General Information

Some of the most handsome species of irises came from the Mediterranean and Central Asia. The Greeks, impressed by their stunning range of colors, named the plant *iris*, after the Greek goddess of the rainbow.

Most scholars agree that the iris could be one of the "lilies" mentioned in Scripture. No one really knows what varieties of lily were cultivated in the gardens and fields of Palestine. Some authorities suggest that different perennials might apply to individual biblical verses: the red anemone, "lips like lilies" (Song of Solomon 5:13); the iris, "grow as the lily" (Hosea 14:5); and the lotus or water lily, "flowers of lilies" (*see* 1 Kings 7:19).

The ordinary word for a lily in Arabic is *sûsan*; the Hebrew word is *shòshan* or *shoshannah*. Greek translators rendered it *krinon*—a plant that grows beside the water.

Of the over fifty varieties of irises found in Palestine, the most likely to be considered a lily would be the yellow *Iris pseudacorus*. It grows in shallow water and on the margin of streams and pools.

Embroidery Suggestions

Add very little embroidery to the iris design. Quilting will best emphasize the ruffed, deeply rippled petals and the sword-shaped leaves.

The petals are easily recognized as belonging to the iris. Use the *satin stitch* in varying (⅛ to ¼ inch) lengths to represent the darker veins on the fall (the part that hangs down from the base of the blossom).

While their kissing cousins, the bearded irises, come in all the colors of the rainbow, the flag iris has yellow or blue blossoms. (Usually very early blooming plants come in these two colors.)

Floss colors: Yellow flowers and light brown veins. Spring green leaves. Or use brown floss to outline embroider the entire design.

Check with the "General Instructions on Embroidery" (p. 17) for the proper length of thread to use for easier embroidery.

Quilting Suggestions

The iris design is very flowing. Start at the star, with a double length of thread. Quilt toward the center, along the petal, and into the stem area. Scoot down to the base of the leaf. Quilt up to the sharp point, then down the other side and along the bottom.

Scoot through the batting to the fall on the left. Quilt the inside shape first, then the ruffled outline. Do not quilt on top of the embroidered veins.

Continue quilting outward from the center. When you run out of thread, use the second half of the original length. Quilt in the opposite direction. Complete the petal and scoot over to the next one.

To use a long thread that is divided into two smaller lengths for easier quilting means starting without a knot. Refer to the "General Instructions on Quilting" (p. 13) for its additional benefits.

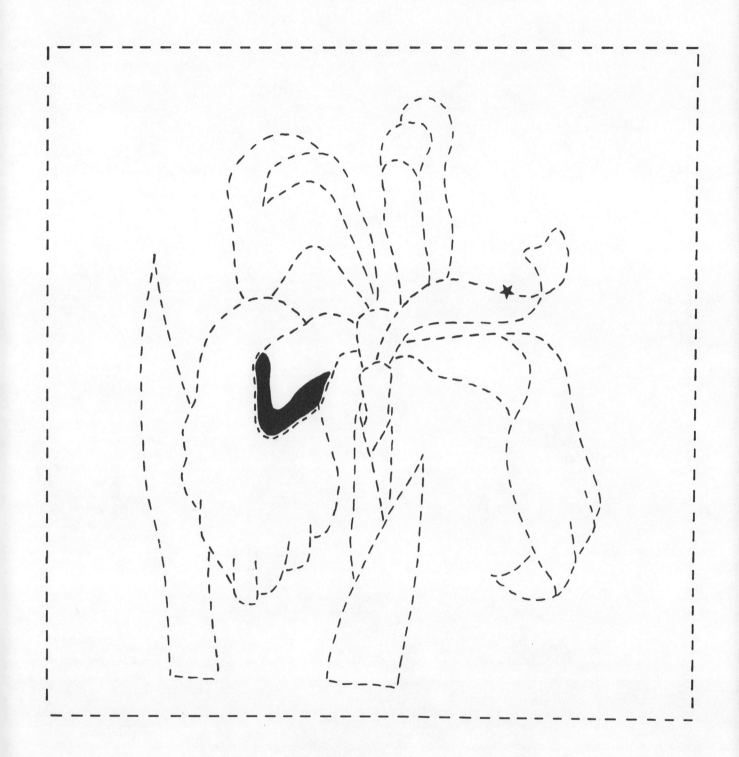

Iris

DETACH PAGE FROM BOOK

For light-colored fabrics—Position pattern under fabric and copy the design in a continuous line.

For darker fabrics—Make a silhouette stencil by copying the pattern on cardboard and cutting out the shape. Position stencil on top of fabric and mark around the designs.

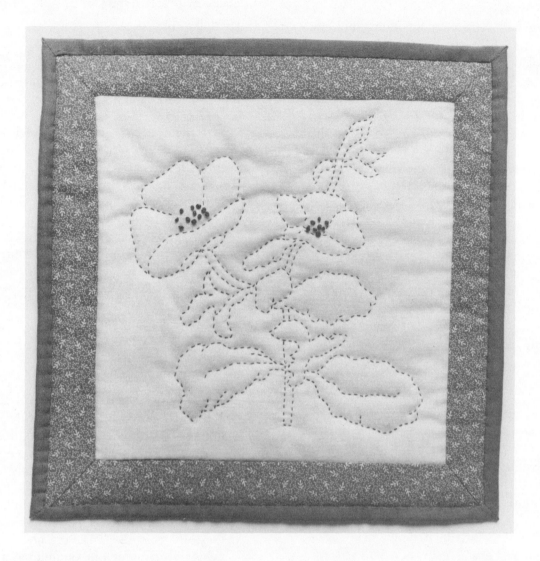

Myrrh

"With myrrh and aloes and cassia your robes are fragrant; from ivory palaces string music brings you joy."

Psalms 45:9 NAB

Latin

Myrrh—*Cictus villosus. Commiphora myrrha,* from the family *Burseraceae.*

Description

Myrrh is derived from small, thorny, flowering trees of the incense-tree family. These stunted, wild-looking shrubs reach a height of from two to three feet. They have odoriferous wood and bark and short, spiney branches.

Three leaflets make up the aromatic leaves, which have such a tightly crinkled texture that they resemble spinach! While the trees have small, white flowers and plumlike fruit, they are primarily cultivated for their resin.

A fragrant, slightly bitter and pungent resin, myrrh exudes from ducts in the branches and stems. The bark splits naturally, or incisions are made to obtain larger amounts of resin.

Myrrh appears as a soft yellowish fluid or gum, which hardens quickly when it drops off the plant. Distilled myrrh is composed of resin, gum, and oil, less than eight percent of the oil makes up the fragrance used in perfumes!

General Information

Once a vital part of a vast and lucrative trading empire dealing in spices and perfumery, myrrh's resinous gum was sold throughout the Near East and Mediterranean regions. It was used as a perfume (Song of Solomon 5:5), as a drug (Mark 15:23), and as an embalming substance (John 19:39).

An essential ingredient in cosmetics (Song of Solomon 3:6) and incenses, myrrh was especially important in the making of anointing oils; and Exodus 30:23 lists it with other fragrant substances.

In biblical times, expensive gifts customarily signified homage. Matthew 2:11 records "Gold, and frankincense, and myrrh" as the costly gifts the wise men of the East gave to the infant Jesus.

Once regarded as rare and precious, myrrh is still valued as a fixative in the making of perfumes. Its antiseptic and astringent properties make it useful in present-day pharmaceutical products.

Embroidery Suggestions

Within the cupped petals, use *French knots* to give shape and definition. The larger flower takes approximately eleven knots, while the smaller one has eight. Scatter as many or as few knots as you prefer, but try to maintain the shape.

If you do not choose to embroider the French knots, use the half moon as a guideline for quilting. Some type of stitching in that area is necessary to give depth to the design.

Myrrh can be further emphasized by using the *outline stitch* for embroidering the entire plant. Refer to the photograph on the album cover (p. 25), made with this design. Purple floss was used throughout. Brown floss, double strand, is also attractive, especially on natural-colored fabric.

Floss colors: Golden centers, white or lavender flowers. Green stems and leaves.

Quilting Suggestions

The star is placed at the center of the design. Start there. The grouping of leaves all but hides the stem. Slightly irregular stitches are necessary to show the ruffled indents of the tightly crinkled leaves.

Completely quilt each petal, one by one, to give movement. There is no possible way to quilt the texture, which looks like crushed velvet.

While this requires a lot of quilting, it is easy quilting. Just zigzag, scooting back and forth from the leaves to the stem to the flowers as they overlap down the block. Each one will puff up nicely.

In a hand-held block, quilt the bud and stem at the top last. Turn the block and remember to keep the backing taut as you quilt toward yourself.

Refer to the "General Instructions on Quilting" (p. 13) for an an explanation of *scooting*.

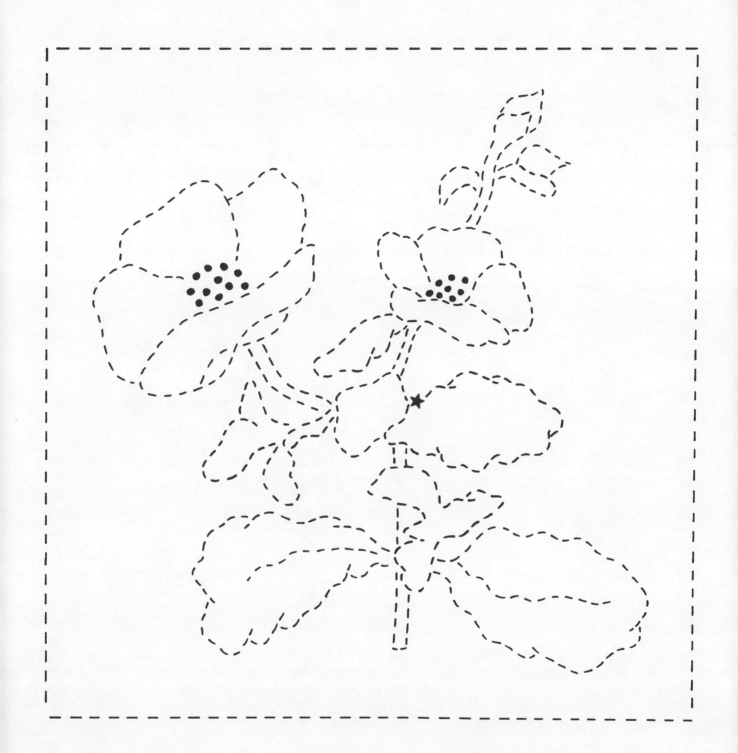

Myrrh

DETACH PAGE FROM BOOK

For light-colored fabrics—Position pattern under fabric and copy the design in a continuous line.

For darker fabrics—Make a silhouette stencil by copying the pattern on cardboard and cutting out the shape. Position stencil on top of fabric and mark around the designs.

Olive

"And he stayed yet other seven days; and again he sent forth the dove out of the ark; And the dove came in to him in the evening; and, lo, in her mouth was an olive leaf pluckt off: so Noah knew that the waters were abated from off the earth."

Genesis 8:10, 11 KJV

Latin

Olive—*Olea europaea*, family *Oleaceae*.

Description

The olive is an evergreen tree, ten to forty feet tall. It is a slow-growing tree, with a thick, twisted trunk and many branches. Some trees live hundreds of years and some as long as a thousand years!

Its leaves, leathery and lanced shaped, are dark green on the top and silvery gray underneath. They grow opposite each other on the stem.

The white flowers (*not shown*), borne in loose clusters, each have four sepals and petals. Its small, fleshy, oval fruit has a stony seed inside. The fruits are either harvested in the green and unripe stage or when they mature to a dark purple or black color.

General Information

Deuteronomy 20:19 says: ". . . Thou shalt not destroy the trees . . . (for the tree of the field is man's life) . . ."

One of the most beautiful and certainly one of the most valuable of all Bible trees, the olive provides man with food, oil, and shelter. Its patient growth sets a pattern for a future of peace and prosperity. With time and work, its beauty (Hosea 14:6) and fruitfulness (Isaiah 17:6; 24:13) seem unending.

The Bible often refers to the olive. Its characteristic growing habits illustrated the point the narrator wanted to make: from the family blessed with children in Psalms 128:3, to Paul's metaphor for Jews and Gentiles in Romans 11:17–24. Because this ancient tree was easily recognized and truly respected, the writers of the Scriptures constantly mentioned it.

The olive is best known as a symbol of peace (Genesis 8:11). Its branches and leaves, along with the dove, have become its universal emblem.

Embroidery Suggestions

The stems from which the cluster of olives grow have been embroidered with the *outline stitch*.

The *satin stitch* emphasizes the shape of one leaf. Here again, choose to use as much or as little embroidery as you like. You can highlight each fruit, leaf, or the entire branch.

Floss colors: Olive green, the yellowish-green color of the unripened fruit, or a dark purple to represent the mature fruit from which oil is extracted.

The leaves are dark green or a silvery-gray shade (for the underside). Use brown for the stems and branch, or to embroider the complete design.

Refer to the "General Instructions on Embroidery" (p. 17) for how-to directions, supplies, and a chart of recommended stitches.

Quilting Suggestions

The star is placed at the tip of one leaf. Begin to quilt there. Use a double length of quilting thread to start. Use the first half to quilt down the leaf, along the stem and to scoot under the olive and leaves to the branch.

Continue to quilt the other two stems and their leaves. Use the second half of your original thread to finish quilting around the leaf. Strive for sharp points on each of these lancelike leaves.

If you do not embroider the stems of the olive cluster, then quilt them. Follow the darker lines. Do not quilt along any embroidered stem!

Take one small stitch at a time when quilting the olive's oval shape. To lock in as much fullness as possible, keep the back fabric taut.

The reason for starting and ending without knots is explained in the "General Instructions on Quilting" (p. 13).

Olive

DETACH PAGE FROM BOOK

For light-colored fabrics—Position pattern under fabric and copy the design in a continuous line.

For darker fabrics—Make a silhouette stencil by copying the pattern on cardboard and cutting out the shape. Position stencil on top of fabric and mark around the designs.

Pomegranate

"For the Lord thy God will bring thee into a good land, of brooks and of waters and of fountains: in the plains of which and the hills deep rivers break out. A land of wheat, and barley, and vineyards, wherein fig trees and pomegranates, and oliveyards grow: a land of oil and honey."

Deuteronomy 8:7, 8 DOUAY

Latin

Pomegranate—fruit of *Punica granatum.*

Description

Pomegranate refers to both the small, shrub-like tree and its fruit. The plants grow from twelve to twenty feet tall, have bright-green, lance-shaped leaves and thorns. Flowers resemble bells, are orange red in color, and are borne toward the ends of the branchlets. The tough calyx lobes protect the petals.

The pomegranate fruit is a berry. It is large, about the size of an orange, but with a smooth, leathery skin. Colors range from brownish yellow to purple or the more familiar scarlet red.

The hard rind contains clusters of juicy seeds deeply imbedded in a soft, reddish pink pulp. They have an acid, agreeable taste—very refreshing.

General Information

The pomegranate is indigenous to the Arabian Peninsula and neighboring countries. Since earliest times it has occupied a position of importance alongside the grape and the fig. Scripture includes numerous references to these three: Numbers 13:23; Deuteronomy 8:8; and Haggai 2:19, to mention a few.

The fruit and flowers of the pomegranate symbolized profusion and fertility. Its prominence in Palestine is indicated by its repeated use as a decoration on holy garments (Exodus 28:33, 34) and as embellishments on important buildings (1 Kings 7:18, 20, 42).

Still cultivated for its fruit and a wine made from its juices, the pomegranate is also a natural dye used for leathers and carpets. This well-known and respected plant symbolizes spring (Song of Solomon 6:11; 7:12).

Embroidery Suggestions

Some embroidery should be added to give texture to the pomegranate design: The thorns along the branches are too spikey to be quilted, therefore, a *straight stitch* is necessary for authenticity.

The petals grow crumpled in the bud, so that a few *French knots* can give dimension to the tightly curled blossoms.

If additional embroidery is desired, try the *satin stitch* to emphasize part of the larger leaves. You can always embroider the entire design using the *outline stitch* with a double strand of brown floss.

Floss colors: Bright green for the leaves, brown for the branches and thorns, vivid reds and scarlets for the fruit and flowers.

See the "General Instructions on Embroidery" (p. 17) for more suggestions.

Quilting Suggestions

The fullness of the round pomegranate just cries out to be quilted first! If held by hand, turn the block sideways. Start your needle at the first star, on the fruit. Use a long thread. Leave two-thirds of the length at that star, and scoot through the batting to the second star on the branch.

This enables you to begin with no knots and at the places best suited to give movement to the design. Refer to the "General Instructions on Quilting" (p. 13) for the benefits of using this technique.

Quilt down the top side of the branch first, remembering to scoot under the curve of the fruit. Scoot off at the bottom to end. Thread your needle again at the first star, now quilt around the entire pomegranate. End off with sharp quilting stitches to give the zigzag effect as shown.

Using new thread, quilt the underside of the branch, starting opposite the second star. *Do not go back up the underside from the left*. Quilt in the same direction. This prevents tugging the fabric on the back, left then right. You can see the difference in pieces of quilting held by hand.

Quilt the entire design except the embroidered thorns and the middle of the leaves. Too much detail quilting flattens this design.

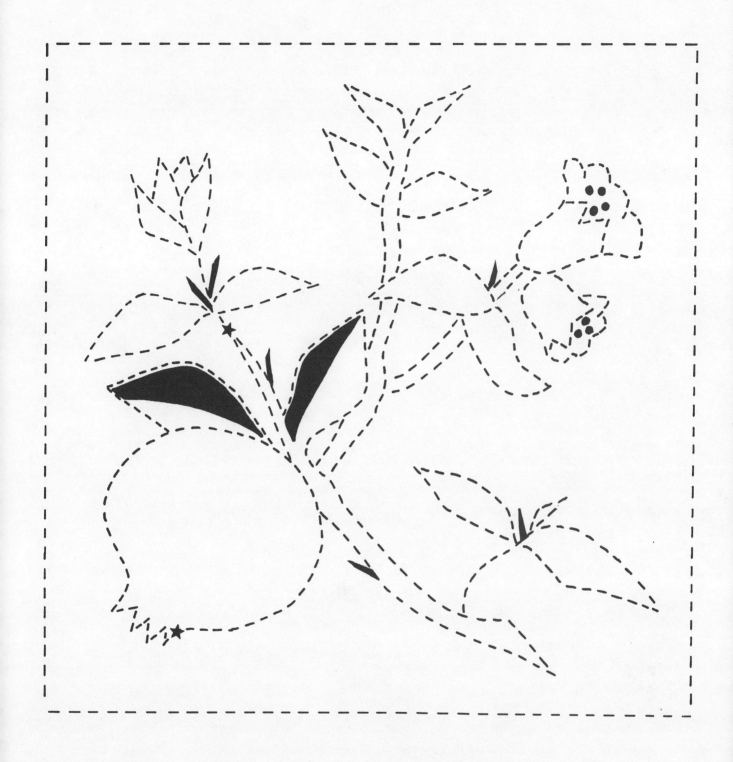

Pomegranate

DETACH PAGE FROM BOOK

For light-colored fabrics—Position pattern under fabric and copy the design in a continuous line.

For darker fabrics—Make a silhouette stencil by copying the pattern on cardboard and cutting out the shape. Position stencil on top of fabric and mark around the designs.

Sweet Storax

"They then sat down to their meal. Looking up, they saw a caravan of Ishmaelites coming from Gilead, their camels laden with gum, balm, and resin to be taken down to Egypt."

Genesis 37:25 NAB

Latin

Storax—*Styrax officinalis* from the family *Styracaceae*.

Description

The storax is a beautiful shrub that sometimes reaches the size of a small tree, ten to twenty feet tall. It has simple, smooth leaves arranged alternately along the stems and bears slender petaled white flowers in spikes of three or four. The tree is very showy when in bloom and resembles a snowdrop bush.

Sweet storax exudes a fragrant balsam from the bark. The yield may be increased by making incisions in the stem and branches. The stacte, oozing out in gummy drops, was sometimes called perfumed tears.

General Information

To ferret out the connections between the Latin names of this plant's genus and the translations of the Hebrew name *nātāph*, you would have to be a scholar of the Scriptures.

Storax, stacte or strakes, and balm can conceivably refer to the same plant or its derivatives! The names are interchangeable, and they all seem to mean the tall shrub or the sweet-smelling drops of resin gum it exudes.

Very fragrant, storax has the scent of vanilla. It is one of the four aromatic ingredients in the holy incense that was made from ". . . sweet spices, stacte, and onycha, and galbanum . . . with pure frankincense . . ." (Exodus 30:34 KJV; *see also* Sirach 24:15 in the apocrypha).

In their caravans traveling from Israel to Egypt, spice merchants carried this scarce and valuable commodity (Genesis 37:25). The gum was highly prized as a perfume and as a medicinal substance.

Embroidery Suggestions

There are several different embroidery stitches used in the sweet storax block.

The full-faced blossom has four *French knots* to give dimension.

The side view of the flower uses the *straight stitch*, to show the stamens poking out from the petals. The *outline stitch* accents the veins on two leaves. Use the *satin stitch* to fill in the receptacles or bases of the flowers.

If you want to minimize the amount of work, eliminate the embroidery on the leaves and bases, but do keep the emphasis on the flowers.

For maximum effect, embroider the above, then use the *outline stitch* around the entire design.

Floss colors: white or light yellow for the flowers and green for leaves and stems. It always looks attractive to use solid brown embroidery floss, double strand, for the entire quilt.

Refer to the "General Instructions on Embroidery" (p. 17) for how-to directions, supplies, and a chart of recommended stitches.

Quilting Suggestions

Begin quilting at the star, with a double length of quilting thread. Quilt down the stem, remembering to scoot under the leaves. Use the second half of the thread to quilt around the front view flower. Quilt down the side of the wide stem, then along the narrower stems into the leaves. Quilt the petals one by one. Do not quilt the top of the bases or around the stamens.

If you choose to embroider the veins on the leaves, do not quilt alongside them. If you did not embroider the veins, quilt the dark lines of the veins for accent.

Refer to the "General Instructions on Quilting" (p. 13) for the benefits of using a quilting frame or hoop for your project.

NEW BRUNSWICK

SASKATCHEWAN

NORTHWEST TERRITORIES

NOVA SCOTIA

ONTARIO

MANITOBA

WFOUNDLAND

TISH COLUMBIA

N TERRITORY

PRINCE
ARD ISLAND

QUEBEC

ALBERTA

O CANADA

O Canada! Our home and native land!
True patriot love in all thy sons command.
With glowing hearts we see thee rise,
The True North strong and free!
From far and wide, O Canada,
We stand on guard for thee.
God keep our land glorious and free!
O Canada, we stand on guard for thee.
O Canada, we stand on guard for thee.

TERRE-NEUVE

COLOMBIE-BRITANNIQUE

TERRITOIRE DU YUKON

ÎLE-DU-PRINCE-EDOUARD

QUÉBEC

ALBERTA

NOUVEAU-BRUNS

SASKATCHEW.

TERRITOIRES
DU NORD-OUE

NOUVELLE-ÉCO

ONTARI

MANITOB.

O CANADA

O Canada! Terre de nos aïeux,
Ton front est ceint de fleurons glorieux!
Car ton bras sait porter l'épée,
Il sait porter la croix!
Ton histoire est une épopée
Des plus brillants exploits.
Et ta valeur, de foi trempée,
Protégera nos foyers et nos droits,
Protégera nos foyers et nos droits,

Gracieuseté

THE OTTAWA
Citizen

Sweet Storax

DETACH PAGE FROM BOOK

For light-colored fabrics—Position pattern under fabric and copy the design in a continuous line.

For darker fabrics—Make a silhouette stencil by copying the pattern on cardboard and cutting out the shape. Position stencil on top of fabric and mark around the designs.

PROJECT
WORKSHEETS
AND
PATTERNS

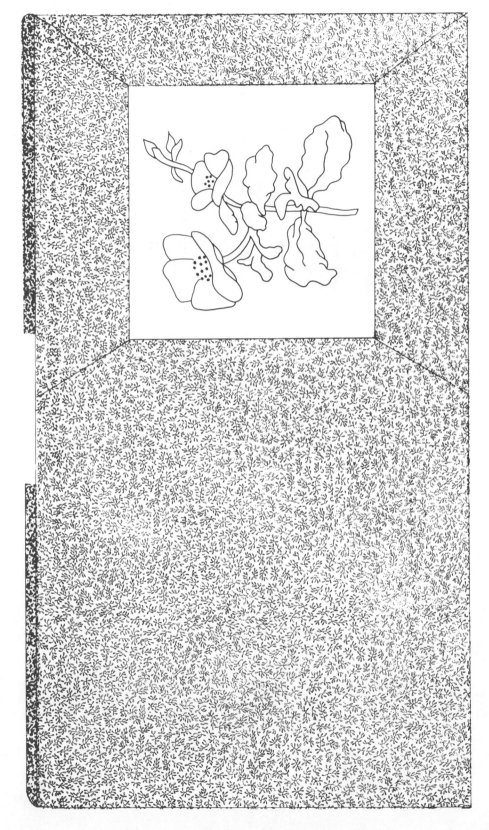

Figure 3—Album cover 21″ x 12″

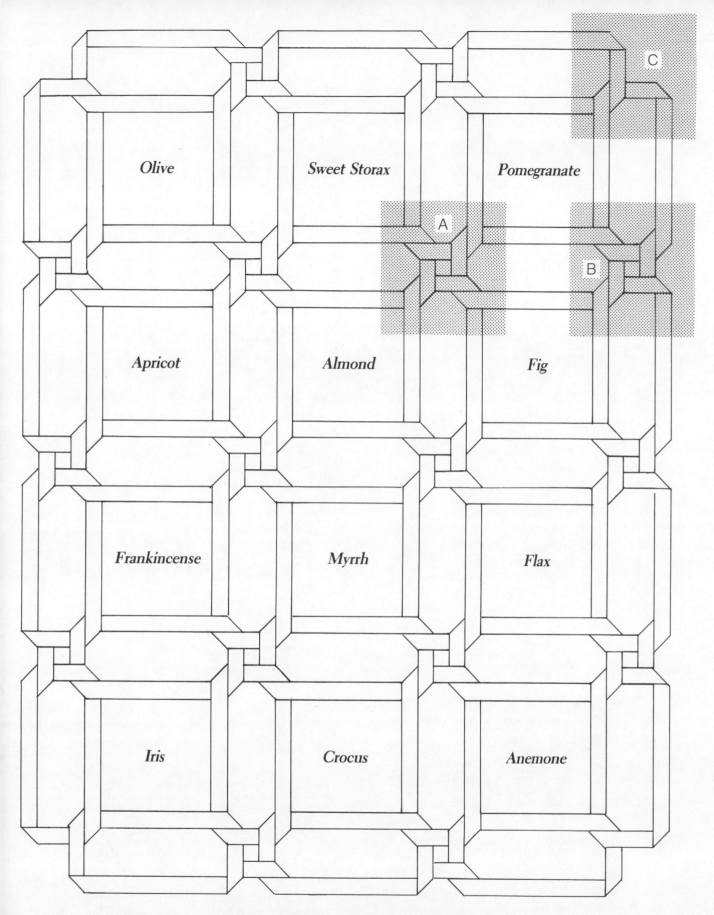

Figure 4—Wall-Hanging Worksheet 42″ x 54″

The Everlasting Chain quilting design is composed of three patterns: A—Intersection, B—Borders, and C—Corner. To mark, detach the following three pages of patterns from the book and refer to the worksheet for proper positioning.

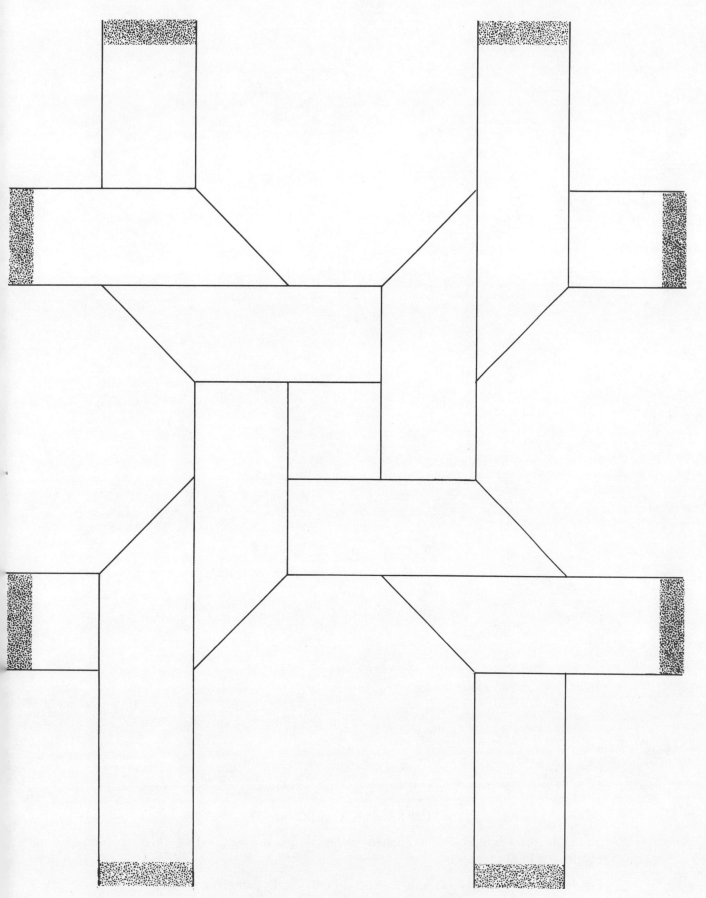

Figure 4A—Intersection Pattern for Everlasting Chain

Extend shaded areas to meet the next section.

DETACH PAGE FROM BOOK

For light-colored fabrics—Position pattern under fabric and copy the design in a continuous line.

For darker fabrics—Make a silhouette stencil by copying the pattern on cardboard and cutting out the shape. Position stencil on top of fabric and mark around the designs.

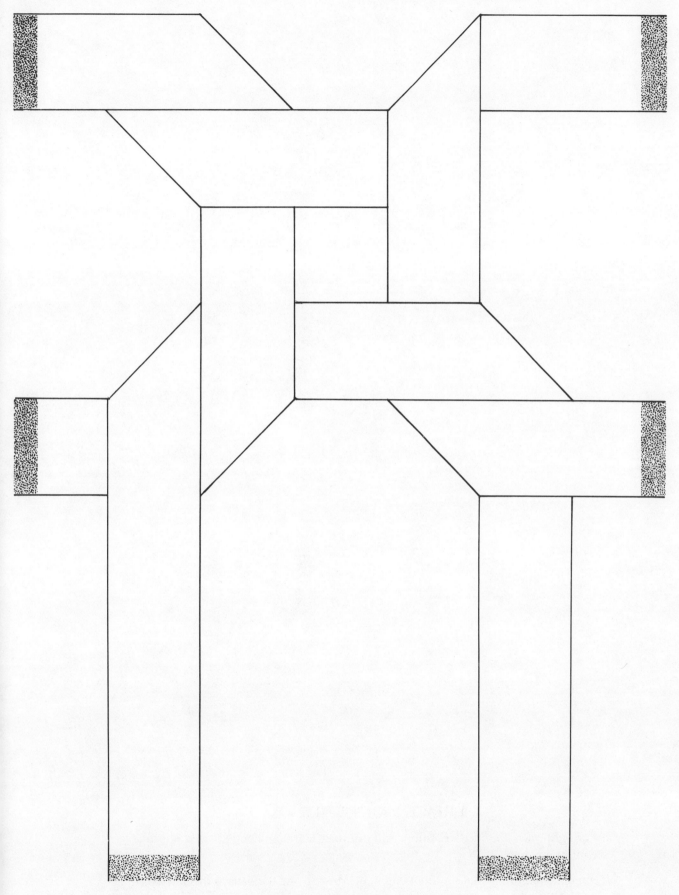

Figure 4B—Border Pattern for Everlasting Chain

Position chain around edges. Lengthen as needed to connect with the other sections.

DETACH PAGE FROM BOOK

For light-colored fabrics—Position pattern under fabric and copy the design in a continuous line.

For darker fabrics—Make a silhouette stencil by copying the pattern on cardboard and cutting out the shape. Position stencil on top of fabric and mark around the designs.

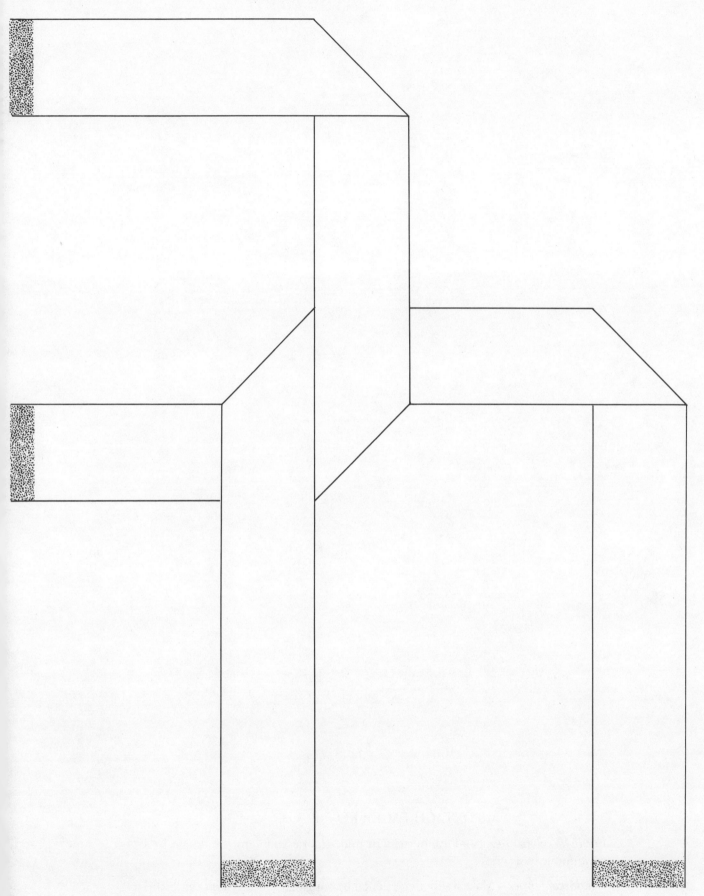

Figure 4C—Corner Pattern for Everlasting Chain

Use for all four corners. Rotate the pattern as shown in worksheet (Figure 4, on p. 81).

DETACH PAGE FROM BOOK

For light-colored fabrics—Position pattern under fabric and copy the design in a continuous line.

For darker fabrics—Make a silhouette stencil by copying the pattern on cardboard and cutting out the shape. Position stencil on top of fabric and mark around the designs.

FINISHING THE QUILT EDGES

Twelve different methods

1. **Narrow bias binding**
   Single-fold bias tape in contrasting color.
   Mark finished size. Baste close to edge.
   Trim layers. Attach tape by piecing on back
   and appliquéing on top.

2. **Wide bias binding**
   Double-fold bias tape in matching color.
   Baste ¼ inch from edge first. Trim fabrics
   and batting. Attach tape by piecing on top,
   hemming in back.

3. **Slip stitched clean edge**
   Mark finished size on all layers. Trim. Tuck
   under top and fold back over batting. Slip
   stitch closed. Use on curved edges.

4. **Top stitched clean edge**
   Mark top with finishing line. Press seams
   under. Fold backing over batting. Pin layers
   together and quilt along edges.

5. Inserted trim
Color coordinated cord piping.
Mark finished size. Sew trim along line, overlapping on side. Cut back bigger, to wrap over batting. Slip stitch along trim.

6. Top fabric wrap
Adds color to quilt back.
Cut backing and batt to finished size. Mark front edge and allow extra to wrap around to back. Turn under seams, miter corners, and hem.

7. Back fabric wrap without quilting
Adds color to front.
Mark and cut top and batting to finished size. Bring backing around to front to form a wide band. Miter corners. Hem.

8. Back fabric wrap with quilting
Adds wider fabric border to front of quilt.
Trim top. Mark and trim batting to any width. Wrap larger backing around batt, miter corners, and hem. Quilt along border.

9. **Bias-looking edge with hem and quilt stitch**
Mark and cut top and batt to size. Bring white backing around to front. Tuck and fold to narrow width. Use quilting thread in all-in-one "hem and quilt" stitch.

10. **Narrow edging with hem and quilt stitch**
Saves a trip around the quilt!
Same as above but the quilting thread has to match the fabric color, to sew with the "hem and quilt" technique.

11. **Back fabric edging with color trim**
Adds accent color without extra sewing.
Mark finished size. Baste folded bias tape on top. Use the "hem and quilt" to catch trim in place.

12. **Blind stitched and quilted top**
For use with darker fabrics.
Mark top smaller than finished size. Tuck under seams. Wrap larger back around trimmed batting. Miter corners. Use matching quilting thread in combination "blind stitch and quilt" finish.

GROUP QUILTING

Group Quilting
For Fun and Fund Raising

Once you've had some experience on the projects in this book, you'll be ready to move on, to a larger project—like a full-fledged quilt. Perhaps you'd like to do one with a group.

The famous, historical quilting bees brought women together for many pleasant hours of social exchange. It still does that today! You, too, can take this delightfully rewarding work and create a program specifically geared to the needs of your church, women's club, or other organization. *Form a quilt group!* It can be educational, socially stimulating, psychologically rewarding, produce tangible items to keep or sell, and afford a continuing source of fund raising.

Consider: A completed quilt can be raffled, auctioned, donated, or presented. It can be sold, displayed, or given away. One midwestern town even holds a yearly Quilt Bingo, and the lucky winners go home with handmade quilts as prizes!

The following guidelines for scheduling quilting events are a result of my experience. This practical advice comes from years of teaching quilting to large groups of women, and showing them how to work together as a team.

To work on bigger projects, especially quilts, you'll need an organized program or "plan of action." You should also realize your goal within a given amount of time. Two months is ideal. That allows enough time to accomplish a goal and still keeps your members' interest.

Action Plan

Week one: Social get-together

Invite your membership to an open meeting— a "show and tell" session in which they bring their own Plants of the Holy Land projects, family quilts, or heirlooms. If possible, have a knowledgeable person give a talk on the history of quilting. The purpose is to excite the people and have them sign up to participate in the program.

Tell everyone what to expect and what they are going to make or achieve. Discuss the cost. Either budget an amount from the group's treasury or divide the sum of the cost of the materials by the number of people involved.

Week two: Planning committee

There is always a nucleus of enthusiastic workers in any organization. You need an experienced person to take charge. Other volunteers have to handle the physical arrangements: Decide who will choose where and when to hold the program, who is responsible for the lights, heat, chairs, and who handles the money. Someone has to coordinate any paperwork or registrations and collect monies due.

One person has to have the final decisions on the project, but the committee should establish the end use of the quilt or its proceeds.

Week three: How-to instructions

Practice patchwork by learning the different techniques of quiltmaking: using a pattern or template; working with the proper grains of the fabric; pressing, marking, and *sewing uniform 1/4-inch seam allowances.* On a group quilt this is the single most important skill!

Basic nine-patch designs are good for beginners and available from any quilting source. The students keep their own practice block. Future sessions will show them how to batt-up, quilt, and finish off the block. They can bring their own fabric, or the group can provide the supplies for this hands-on learning experience.

Week four: Preparation

A smaller work committee designs the group quilt. They decide on the colors (earth tones, blues or browns are best-sellers), select and buy the fabrics, and make the patterns. They are responsible for cutting out the quilt accurately.

Quilts with a theme have more meaning to the group. Some examples are:

"Children's Delight"—nursery school
"Steps to the Altar"—confirmation class
"Oakleaves"—Oakland High School
"Jacob's Ladder"—Minister's anniversary

For more quilt ideas, refer to: *Creative American Quilting Inspired by the Bible,* by Suzzy Chalfant Payne and Susan Aylsworth Murwin

(Old Tappan, N.J.: Fleming H. Revell Co., 1982).

A word of advice—after cutting out the quilt, package all the pieces necessary for one block in a plastic bag. This prevents loss or duplication of pieces when handed out to the individual sewers.

Week five: Making a group quilt

The homework assignment, the nine-patch practice block, is brought back to the meeting and *checked for accuracy*. The benefit of a group quilt is having many people share in the work. However, to be a success the finished work has to look as if only one person sewed it! That means uniform seams, identical appliqué stitches, and matching patchwork.

Give out the precut pieces of the group quilt and very carefully go over the directions for assembling the pieces, step by step. Any printed sketch with easy instructions would be helpful.

Week six: Work session

Referring to a worksheet that shows the quilt design, layout, and measurements, start joining each completed block into the quilt. Attach blocks in rows, then rows into strips.

Depending on the design, you may need to add sashing or borders. One small group of four women can sew the long seams of the backing fabric. All work should be pressed as assembled.

Now is the time to learn how to quilt. Each student needs batting, a backing square, and quilting sewing supplies. Read the "General Instructions on Quilting" (p. 13) for suggestions. Quilting practice is done at home at each person's leisure. The quilted block can be made into a placemat, pillow, or tote bag. Some samples of completed items should be shown to the group.

The members are encouraged to finish their project and bring it to the quilting bee.

Week seven: Getting ready to quilt

A small work committee is again needed to prepare the quilt for the quilting frame. All the blocks should have been joined together and the final sewing details completed. Now an experienced quilter needs to supervise preparing the quilt to put it on the frame: the final pressing, trimming of loose threads, marking the quilting design, and layering of the textile sandwich (the backing, batting, and the quilt top).

Attach the basted quilt to the frame. It is best to use a large upright frame for the quilting bee. Its size permits maximum participation by the group members.

Week eight: The quilting bee

This is a social event that lasts from four to six hours. Refreshments are always welcomed by the quilters. Schedule small groups to arrive at staggered time intervals so that each person can have ample space to quilt at the frame.

The quilting design can vary from premarked cables to quick, quilt-in-the-ditch quilting. Adjust the quilting time schedule according to the degree of difficulty. If time and place are no problem, continue the bee for more than one day. The secret is to relax and enjoy yourself while you admire the handwork.

The completed projects can be displayed at a "bring and brag" table. Invite family and friends to visit during the quilting bee. Maybe they will sign up for the next event!

Later: Finishing the edges

When the quilting is completed, take the quilt off the frame and allow it to rest flat. Tidy up any tails or threads and get ready to finish the edges. Choose from any of the twelve finishing methods listed on pp. 90—92.

Special attention should be given to the corners; they must be square and mitered if possible. Check that the quilt is clean, neat, and in a saleable condition.

Start planning your next quilt!

BIBLIOGRAPHY

Butler, Anne. *The Arco Encyclopedia of Embroidery Stitches*. New York: Arco Publishing, 1979.

Crockett, James Underwood. *Time-Life Encyclopedia of Gardening*. Alexandria, Va.: Time-Life Books, 1972.

Davis, J. D. *Dictionary of the Bible*. Westwood, N.J.: Fleming H. Revell, 1924.

Everett, T. H., ed. *New Illustrated Encyclopedia of Gardening*. New York: Greystone Press.

Hadfield, Miles. *Everyman's Wild Flowers and Trees*. London: J. M. Dent, 1957.

Hersey, Jean. *Wild Flowers to Know and Grow*. Princeton, N.J.: D. Van Nostrand, 1964.

Johnson, Marjorie P., comp. *Concise Encylopedia of Favorite Flowers*. Edited by Montague Free. Garden City, N.Y.: Doubleday, 1953.

McCurdy, Robert M., arr. *Book of Garden Flowers*. New York: Doubleday, Doran, 1931.

New Encyclopedia Britannica. Chicago: Encyclopedia Britannica, 1974.

Reader's Digest Editors. *Reader's Digest Atlas of the Bible*. Pleasantville, N.Y.: Reader's Digest Assoc., 1981.

Reader's Digest Editors. *Reader's Digest Complete Guide to Needlework*. Pleasantville, N.Y.: Reader's Digest Assoc., 1979.

Untermeyer, Louis. *Plants of the Bible*. New York: Golden Press.

Wilson, Adelaide B. *Flower Arrangement for Churches*. New York: M. Barrows, 1952.